This book is for me, but more specifically for
the kid I used to be and all the others like him.
The world is a huge and endlessly fascinating place
so never lose your sense of wonder.
—B.R.

Tilbury House Publishers, an imprint of Cherry Lake Publishing Group
Ann Arbor, Michigan
www.tilburyhouse.com

First US edition 2023
ISBN: 978-1-6689-3682-5

Original English language edition first published by Ladybird Books Ltd, 20 Vauxhall Bridge Road, London, SW1V 2SA, UK
Copyright © Ben Rothery, 2022
The moral right of the author/illustrator has been asserted. All rights reserved.
Zoological consultant: Dr. Nick Crumpton

Printed in China
A CIP catalog record for this book is available from the British Library
ISBN: 978–0–241–53229–4

## Measurements

You'll see a few metric measurements in this book. Metric measurements are used in most of the world, but a few countries (including the US) still use the Imperial system of inches, feet, ounces, and pounds. Here are some conversion formulas to get from one system to the other.

### Length

To convert meters to feet, multiply by 3.281. To convert centimeters to inches, divide by 2.54.

- 1 meter (or metre) = 39.37 inches, or about 3 feet; 1 foot = 0.305 meter; 1 yard = 0.914 meter.
- 1 centimeter (or centimetre) = 0.39 inch, less than half an inch; 1 inch = 2.54 centimeters.
- 1 millimeter = 0.039 inch; 1 inch = 25.4 millimeters.
- 1 kilometer = 0.62 mile; 1 mile = 1.609 kilometers.

### Weight/Mass

To convert grams to ounces, divide by 28.35. To convert kilograms to pounds, multiply by 2.205.

- 1 gram = 0.035 ounce; 1 ounce = 28.35 grams.
- 1 kilogram = 2.205 pounds; 1 pound = 0.454 kilogram; 1 ton = 2,000 pounds or 907 kilograms; 1 metric ton = 1,000 kilograms.

BEN ROTHERY'S

# Weird
### AND
# Wonderful
# Animals

TILBURY HOUSE PUBLISHERS

# Contents

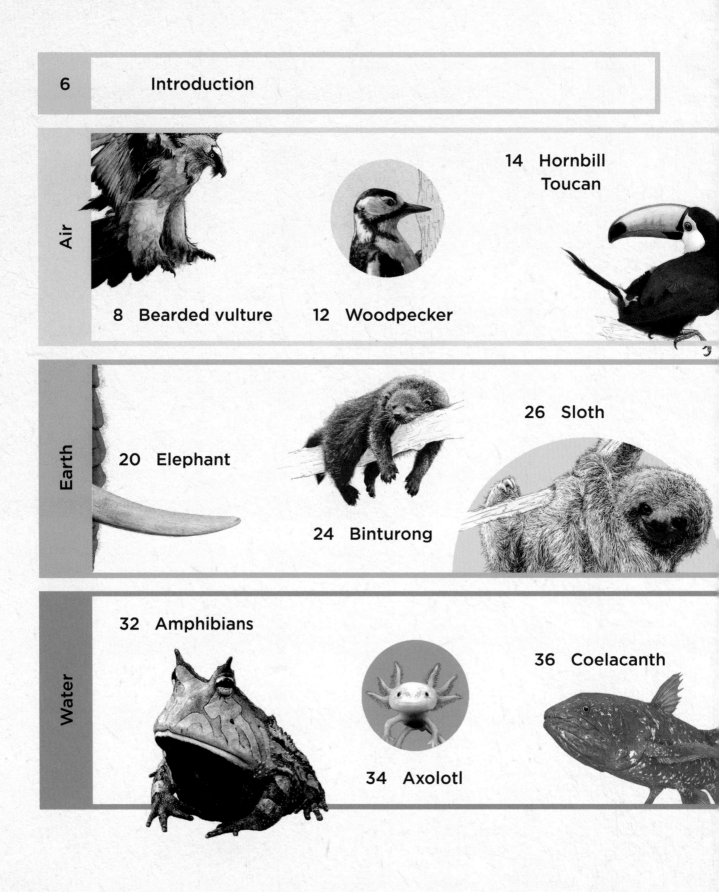

3

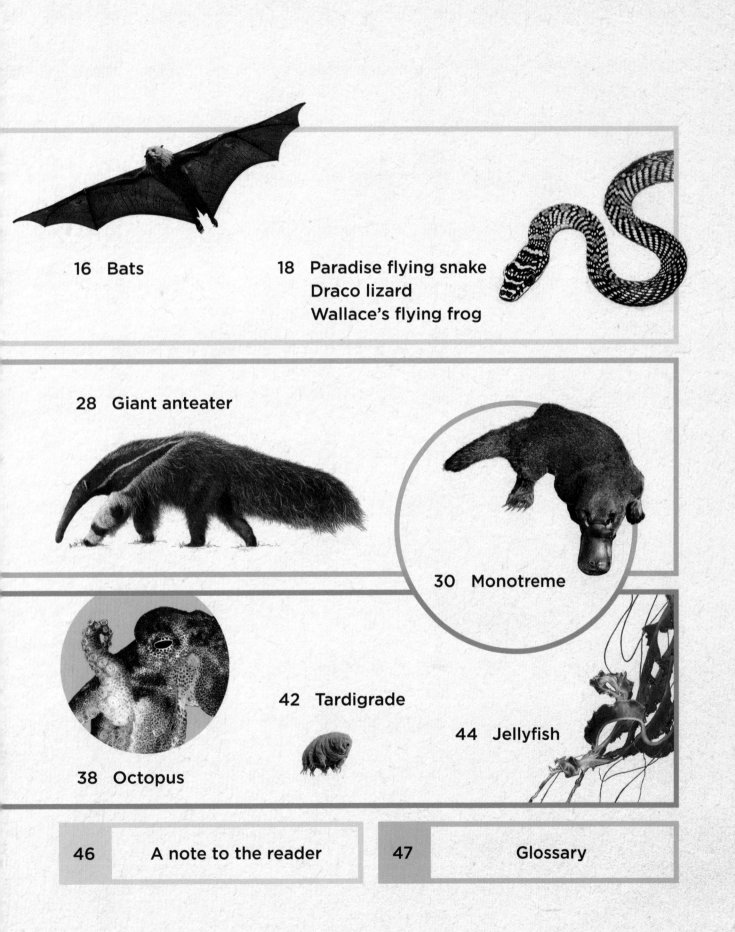

# Introduction

Planet Earth is home to a great many weird animals, some of which are so strange as to defy belief.

Many only look peculiar on the outside, with too many arms, legs, or eyes, but in others, the weirdness is a little better hidden . . .

In this book, we'll introduce you to some of the most bizarre **species*** with whom we share our home. We'll look at what makes them so strange, why they are the way they are, why they do the things they do, and we'll even inspect some species that don't seem strange on the surface at all.

And while this is by no means a complete list, I hope this book will provide you with a glimpse of the amazing variety of shapes, colors, and behaviors that go into making our planet's animals so weird and so wonderful.

*Ben Rothery*

*Definitions of words in **bold** can be found in the glossary on page 47.

7

# Bearded vulture / lammergeier
*Gypaetus barbatus*

**Location: Europe, Asia, and Africa**
**Length: 37-49.2 inches (94-125 centimeters)**
**Wingspan: 7.7-9.2 feet (231-281 cm)**
**Weight: 8.8-15.5 pounds (4-7 kilograms)**

Once found in mountain ranges from Spain to South Africa and France to Tibet, the bearded vulture is now sadly **extinct** in many places it historically called home.

Lammergeier means "lamb vulture" in German, and people have mistakenly blamed this magnificent bird for carrying off livestock and even children – but the reality is far stranger. Although it will occasionally eat live **prey**, the bearded vulture is the only animal that feeds almost exclusively on bones, preferring them to all other food sources.

From a young age, the bearded vulture is able to snap and swallow smaller pieces of whole bone, but it can take up to seven years to master the skills it needs to eat larger bones. First, the bird drops the larger bones from great heights so they smash apart. Then, once it has eaten the pieces, they are digested by its powerful stomach acid.

A lammergeier's grooming ritual is also extraordinary. It takes luxurious baths in sulphur springs rich in **chemicals** including iron oxide, which leaves the bird's shoulders, neck, and chest red and bronzed. No one is entirely sure why bearded vultures do this, but some scientists believe the iron oxide helps keep the birds' feathers free of harmful diseases – an ever-present threat to the life of a **scavenger**.

# Woodpecker
*Picinae*

**Location: worldwide, except Australasia, Antarctica, and the Arctic**
**Length: 3-19.7 in (7.5-50.0 cm)**
**Weight: 8.8-14.2 ounces (250-400 grams)**

There are approximately two hundred species of woodpecker around the world, and while they vary in size, color and pattern, they share the same amazing features and behaviors. Woodpeckers are named after their habit of drumming their beaks into trees to find food, dig nest holes, and communicate with one another.

To get at the insects it eats, the woodpecker possesses two useful features. The first is its self-sharpening, chisel-shaped beak, which it uses to hammer holes. The second is its long tail, which it stiffens to brace itself against a tree while it is drilling.

A woodpecker pecks nearly twenty times per second, and as many as twelve thousand times per day. This creates a huge force against its small body. So, to avoid knocking itself out, the woodpecker has **evolved** some amazing hidden **adaptations**. Its beak is covered by two layers: a hard outer shell that helps drill into wood, and a spongy inner layer that helps absorb the force of each peck. The two halves of the woodpecker's beak are also slightly different lengths – the upper part overlaps the lower. This sends the force around the sides of the bird's head, rather than through the center.

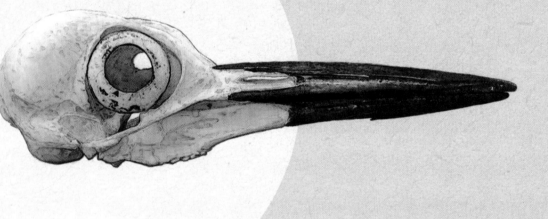

But the woodpecker's weirdest adaptation is its massively long tongue, which is around one-third of the length of the bird. As well as helping it reach insects, the woodpecker's tongue wraps around the inside of its skull, where it acts like a seatbelt for its brain, stopping the brain from shaking around as the bird pecks.

# Hornbill
## *Bucerotidae*

**Location: tropical and subtropical
Africa, Asia, and Melanesia
Length: 1.3-5.3 ft (40-160 cm)
Weight: 4.4-8.8 lb (2-4 kg)**

The most prominent feature of the great
hornbill – other than its large beak – is the
bright yellow-and-black casque (horn) on top
of its beak. Male hornbills use their casques
to butt each other in flight, like charging rams.

# Toucan
*Ramphastidae*

**Location: Central and South America**
**Length: 11.4-25 in (29-63 cm)**
**Weight: 4.5-24 oz (130-680 g)**

Toucans might look a lot like hornbills, but the two are not closely related. Instead, their similarity in appearance – and in behavior – is an example of convergent evolution, which happens when distantly related or even totally unrelated animals evolve similar features. This occurs because they live in similar **habitats**, so they must respond to the same kinds of problems.

Despite their very different locations, the approximately forty species of toucan and sixty species of hornbill mostly live in rainforests. Their diet is mainly fruit, but they will also eat smaller birds, insects, small **mammals**, and reptiles, if they can catch them.

The toco toucan is the largest toucan, and its oversized beak is one-third the length of its body. It uses its beak for many things, including attracting a **mate**, reaching food, wrestling with other toucans, and helping to control its body temperature.

Being so alike, toucans and hornbills find themselves in similar danger. Both amazing bird families are threatened by hunting, habitat loss, deforestation, and the illegal wildlife trade. Many species are listed as **endangered**, some critically so.

# Bats
## *Chiroptera*

**Location: worldwide, except Antarctica and the Arctic**
**Wingspan: 5.9 in-5 ft (15-150 cm)**
**Weight: .7 oz-3.5 lb (2.0 g - 1.6 kg)**

Bats are amazing animals, with more than 1,400 species as weird as they are different from one another. They're the world's only true flying mammal, able to propel themselves through the air thanks to the very thin skin stretched between their feet and long fingers.

Contrary to popular belief, not all bats sleep and rest upside down – although many do. Most aren't blind, either. In fact, only the smaller species use **echolocation** as their main **sense** for navigation and hunting. Larger species rely on their eyesight, which is many times stronger than that of humans.

Native to Mexico, Central America, and South America, vampire bats are very small, with a wingspan of less than one foot (30 cm). They are also completely sanguinivorous, meaning they feed on blood. They are the only mammal species that does this, and they rarely kill the animals they feed off.

The vampire bat has some amazing adaptations for its unusual diet, including three **infrared** sensors located just above its nose. These sensors detect heat and help the bat find blood vessels beneath an animal's skin. The bat's teeth are so sharp that they can pierce the skin without the animal feeling it. Then, a substance in the bat's saliva prevents the animal's blood from **clotting**, allowing the bat to drink its meal from the wound.

# Paradise flying snake
## *Chrysopelea paradisi*

**Location: South East Asia**
**Length: 1.9-4 ft (60-120 cm)**
**Weight: 1-2.2 lb (450 g - 1kg)**

This snake flattens and stiffens its body into an "S" shape in order to glide up to sixty-six feet (twenty meters) between trees in search of food. Although it can't fly, it is able to direct itself by changing the shape and angle of its body as it falls.

# Draco lizard
## *Draco volans*

**Location: South East Asia and southern India**
**Length: 7-7.9 in (18-20 cm)**
**Weight: less than .75 oz (20 g)**

This small, termite-eating lizard has elongated ribs separated by folds of skin. These ribs act like wings when the skin is unfolded, allowing the lizard to glide for nearly two hundred feet (sixty meters) between branches, using its tail to steer.

Despite its small size, the draco lizard is surprisingly aggressive, chasing other lizards and even other animals out of its **territory**.

# Wallace's flying frog
## *Rhacophorus nigropalmatus*

**Location: South East Asia and Indonesia**
**Length: 3-4 in (8-10 cm)**
**Weight: various**

The Wallace's flying frog spends most of its life high in the trees of its rainforest home, coming down only to mate and lay eggs.

It has huge webbed feet that it uses like parachutes to glide up to fifty feet (fifteen meters) between trees – an impressively long way for an animal around 3 - 4 inches (8-10 centimeters) long.

# Elephant
## *Elephantidae*

**Location: Africa and Asia**
**Height: 8.2-13.2 ft  (2.5-4.0 m)**
**Weight: 2-7 tons (1,800-6,300 kg)**

Elephants might not seem especially weird or wonderful, but the world's largest land animal has many strange features across its three species: African savanna, African forest, and Asian.

First, consider the elephant's trunk, which is actually an extra-long nose containing up to forty thousand muscles. Elephants use their trunks not just for smelling and breathing, but also for communicating, drinking, and grabbing things. The African savanna elephant even has two finger-like growths at the tip of its trunk that it uses to grab small items.

Elephants sleep standing up, and although they might look flat-footed, they're actually standing on the tips of their toes – there's a pad of fat and gristle behind their toes to absorb their massive weight. Elephants can also "hear" through their feet, sensing low rumbles caused by other animals up to 20 miles (32 kilometers) away.

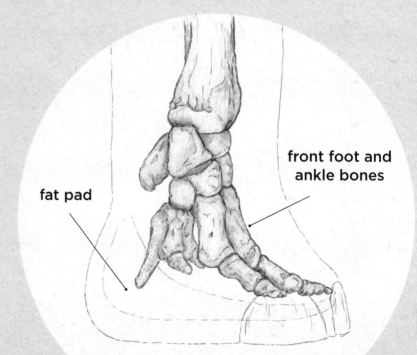

fat pad

front foot and ankle bones

**Opposite: African savanna elephant**

# Asian elephant
## *Elephas maximus*

**Location: widely spread**
**Height: 8.9 ft (2.7 m) (bulls)**
**Weight: 4.4 tons (3,991 kg) (bulls)**

An elephant's sail-like ears aren't just for hearing. They also help cool its large body. In hot weather, the blood supply to the ears increases, and the elephant flaps them around to release body heat.

# African savanna elephant
*Loxodonta africana*

**Location: Africa**
**Height: up to 13.1 ft (4 m)**
**Weight: 7 T (6,300 kg)**

If all that wasn't weird enough, an elephant's tusks are actually very long teeth. They grow constantly throughout an elephant's life, and it uses them to fight and dig for food.

# Binturong
## *Arctictis binturong*

**Location: South East Asia**
**Height: 2.5-3 ft (76-91 cm)**
**Weight: 24.2-70.5 lb (11-32 kg)**

With a face like a cat, a body like a bear, shaggy fur, and stiff white whiskers, this strange animal might be known as a "bearcat," but it isn't closely related to either animal.

Although technically a member of the **Carnivora** group, the binturong is not a **carnivore**. Instead, most of this slow-moving creature's diet consists of fruit and leaves because it spends most of its life high in the trees of its rainforest home.

As well as having strong claws, the binturong can rotate its hind legs backward to keep a strong grip when climbing down trees head first.

Binturongs mate throughout the year, yet they're able to wait and time the birth of their young to a season with favorable conditions. This is a feature called delayed implantation, and only around 1.5 percent of mammals can do it.

If all that wasn't unique enough, binturongs also smell like buttered popcorn. This is because of a substance in their pee called 2-acetyl-1-pyrroline, which they use to mark their territory and attract mates.

# Sloth
*Folivora*

**Location: Central and South America**
**Height: 22.8-26.8 in (58-68 cm)**
**Weight: 15.4-17.6 lb (7-8 kg)**

There are two types of sloth – two-toed and three-toed – divided into six different species. These tree-dwellers spend almost all their lives high in the trees, munching on leaves and twigs, and coming down only once a week to poo.

Many people think that sloths sleep all day, but they actually spend just over nine hours asleep. They also move less than 145 feet (40 meters) a day. Sloths move so slowly that algae grows on their fur, staining them green and adding useful **camouflage**.

**Pygmy three-toed sloth**

Linnaeus's two-toed sloth

Hoffmann's two-toed sloth

Maned sloth

Pale-throated sloth

Brown-throated sloth

Sloths spend enough time upside down that their fur grows in the opposite direction to other mammals'. This also allows rainwater to flow off their bodies. However, three-toed sloths will often wedge themselves upright in branches to eat.

Looks can sometimes be deceptive! The three-toed sloth has more neck bones than most mammals. Even a giraffe has only seven neck vertebrae, but this type of sloth has ten. The extra bones allow three-toed sloths to turn their heads almost completely around, a useful skill to spot incoming danger for such a slow-moving animal.

# Giant anteater
## *Myrmecophaga tridactyla*

**Location: Central and South America**
**Height: 5.9-8.2 ft (1.8-2.5 m)**
**Weight: 72.7-110.2 lb (33-50 kg)**

The giant anteater, also known as the "ant bear," is the largest of the four anteater species. As its name suggests, an anteater's diet consists exclusively of ants, which it gets by tearing into anthills with its powerful front limbs and razor-sharp claws. To keep its claws sharp for feeding and self-defense, the giant anteater walks on its knuckles.

Anteaters are edentate animals, meaning they have no teeth. Instead, they use their long, sticky tongues to eat up to thirty thousand ants per day. They must eat quickly, though, as their prey fight back with painful stings and bites, meaning anteaters can only feed in short bursts. To capture as many ants as they can before they are forced to stop, anteaters flick out their tongues an astonishing one hundred and fifty times every minute.

# Monotreme

There are five species of monotreme divided into two types: the duck-billed platypus and the four species of echidna. In a crowded competition, they probably take the crown for the weirdest land animals.

Although they're mammals, monotremes don't give birth to live young. Instead, they lay eggs like their **reptilian** ancestors. Females feed their infants milk like other mammals do, but they don't have nipples. Instead, they release milk through **glands** on their bellies and their babies lap it up.

Water / Earth

It is toothless and uses a long tongue covered in sticky mucus to catch ants and termites. It can consume up to 4.2 pounds (2 kilograms) in a single meal – that's approximately 285,000 ants!

The echidna looks like a cross between an anteater and a hedgehog.

Strangely, the echidna's hind claws point backward. This is possibly an adaptation to help it dig.

The platypus is found in rivers and lakes throughout eastern Australia and Tasmania. It looks like a cross between a duck, an otter, and a beaver – so it's little surprise that early European scientists didn't even believe it was a real animal!

A platypus spends much of its life underwater, searching along river beds for worms, insects, and shellfish. Although the platypus's beak looks hard, it is actually soft and contains forty thousand special sensors to help the platypus find food in the dark. The platypus has no teeth, so it swallows small bits of shell and gravel with its food to help "chew" it before swallowing.

The male platypus is one of only a very small number of mammals to be **venomous**, possessing spines on its hind feet that it can use to defend itself.

# Amphibians
## *Lissamphibia*

Amphibians are a hugely diverse group of small **vertebrates**, such as frogs and toads, that need either water or a very damp environment to survive.

Amphibians breathe and absorb water through their very thin skin. This skin is special in other ways too: all species have skin glands that produce a range of useful substances. These are used to transport water, **oxygen**, and **carbon dioxide** either into or out of the animal, helping it breathe. Others are used to fight infections or for defense – either as a warning and **toxin**, as with poison dart frogs, or just as a toxin, as with some toads.

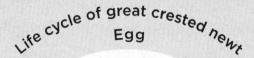

Life cycle of great crested newt
Egg

**Horned frog**
*Ceratophrys calcarata*

Larva of great crested newt

Adult great crested newt

Another weird but amazing feature of most amphibians is their egg–**larva**–adult life cycle. The larvae are **aquatic**, meaning they're free-swimming and breathe through gills. Once they've reached a certain size, the young start to develop limbs and lungs. Some also lose their tails, eventually leaving the water as adults to spend the rest of their lives on land. This process is known as "metamorphosis."

# Axolotl
## *Ambystoma mexicanum*

**Location: Mexico**
**Length: 5.9-17.7 in (15-45 cm)**
**Weight: 2.1-14.1 oz (60-400 g)**

This strange-looking **salamander** never completely outgrows its juvenile stage, retaining its gills and spending its whole life underwater. An adult axolotl also has fully functional lungs and can breathe through its skin.

The strangest thing about the axolotl, however, is its ability to completely regrow lost limbs and heal a damaged heart, spine, and even parts of its brain.

Axolotls are critically endangered in the wild due to water pollution and the introduction of **predators**. There are thought to be only a few hundred wild individuals left living in the canals of Mexico City, which is their only natural habitat.

# Coelacanth
## *Coelacanthiformes*

**Location: Africa and Indonesia**
**Length: 4.9-6.6 ft (1.5-2.0 m)**
**Weight: 99.2-198.4 lb (45-90 kg)**

Coelacanths are mysterious deep-sea fish that spend their days at depths of around 550 yards (500 meters). They are so rare that the group of fish they belong to was thought to have become extinct around 66 million years ago, only rediscovered in 1938 off the coast of South Africa.

The two known species of coelacanth live for sixty years or more, and they evolved into their current forms approximately 400 million years ago.

The coelacanth has two unique features not found in any other living vertebrate. The first is a special sensory organ in its snout that it uses to detect prey. The second is a joint in its skull that allows the front portion of its head to swing upward. This means it can open its mouth much wider to tackle larger prey.

Even the way the coelacanth moves is unusual. It has two pairs of lobe fins, which extend away from its body like legs and move in an alternating pattern, like a trotting horse. This means it can take advantage of different water currents and drift along, using its fins to keep steady as it moves through the water.

Coelacanths also have side fins that flap like wings. As a result, these strange fish can remain very still, doing what looks like headstands for long periods of time. They can even swim upside down.

# Octopus
## *Octopoda*

**Location: worldwide**
**Length: 1 in-3 ft (2.5-90.0 cm)**
**Weight: .03 oz-22 lb (1 g - 10 kg)**

With eight arms, three hearts, no skeleton, and the ability to change color, texture, and shape, the octopus surely qualifies as one of the weirdest animals on Earth.

An octopus has what's known as "blue blood." Where human blood – and blood of nearly all vertebrates – contains a substance called haemoglobin that makes it red, an octopus's blood contains a substance called haemocyanin that makes it blue. Haemocyanin is better at transporting oxygen around the body in cold and low-oxygen conditions, like the ocean.

**Beak**

There are three hundred species of octopus, and these wonderfully intelligent creatures have a great memory but short lifespans. They only live between six months and five years because they die shortly after they **reproduce**. But their survival skills are helped by clever tricks, such as escaping from predators by shooting a sticky cloud of ink out of a muscular tube called a siphon.

An octopus has a central brain between its eyes, but each of its eight arms can move independently of the others. This is thanks to each arm having its own "brain" – really a bundle of **nerves** usually found in a brain, and it helps the arm do some special things. Each arm is also covered with suction cups, which the octopus uses to grip and move objects, catch prey, and even taste what it touches.

Eye

Suction cup

# Greater blue-ringed octopus
## *Hapalochlaena lunulata*

**Location:** Indonesia, the Philippines, Papua New Guinea, Vanuatu, and the Solomon Islands

**Length:** 3.9-4.7 in (10-12 cm) (including arms)

**Weight:** under 4 oz (100 g)

# Tardigrade
## *Tardigradas*

**Location: worldwide**
**Length: 0.01-0.02 in
(0.3-0.5 millimeters)**

Tardigrades are a group of approximately 1,300 species of very tiny eight-legged animals. They are known as "water bears" because they look like little bears. They have been around for nearly 600 million years – that's almost 400 million years before the first dinosaurs.

Although tardigrades are called aquatic animals, they've been found in many different environments, from the deep ocean to the edges of volcanoes.

Despite their tiny size – you need a microscope to see them – tardigrades belong to a category of animals known as "extremophiles," animals that can survive in environments where others can't. You can boil them, freeze them, crush them, and even shoot them into space, and it doesn't matter. Tardigrades are practically indestructible. They can even survive for up to thirty years without food or water.

**Around two hundred tardigrades could fit inside this 1-centimeter circle.**

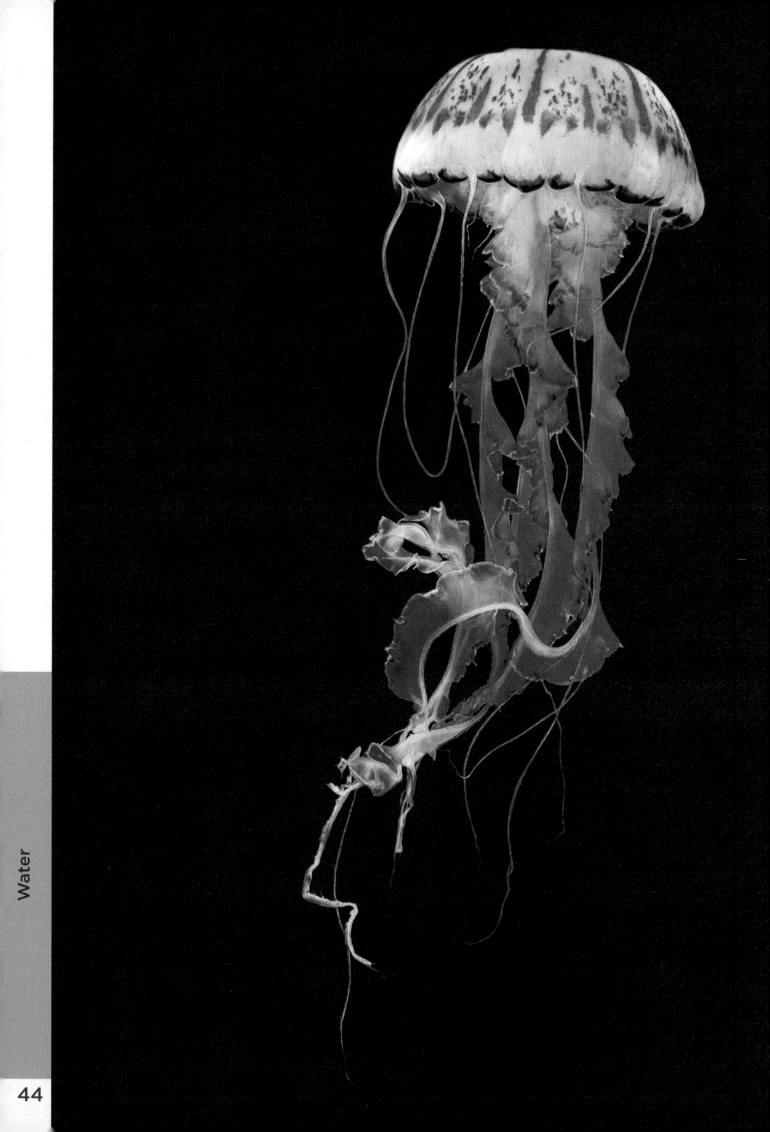

# Jellyfish
## *Medusozoa*

**Location: salt water and fresh water (worldwide)**
**Length: .4 in-11.7 ft (1-360 cm)**
**Weight: .7 oz-441 lb (20 g - 200 kg)**

Jellyfish come in a dazzling array of colors and can have as few as four tentacles or up to hundreds.

Despite having no brain, heart, blood, or bones, many jellyfish are good hunters. They use their stinging tentacles to catch a wide variety of prey, including fish, **crustaceans,** and even other jellyfish.

Being simple creatures, jellyfish don't use their mouths just to eat. They also use them for pooping and to jet water to help propel themselves along. Although they may seem like basic animals, some jellyfish can glow in the dark and others are among the world's deadliest creatures because of their venomous stings.

### Dear reader,

Our world is home to a great many weird and wonderful species – but often what makes an animal weird to us is actually just the way it has adapted to live in a particular place. And, while these adaptations might have allowed some species to survive for millions of years, these same features now leave them vulnerable to the speed at which the world around them is changing. They cannot behave differently or live anywhere else, so when their habitats disappear, they do, too.

Roughly nine million animal species call Planet Earth home, and these creatures come in every shape, size, and color you could imagine. They are what make our world truly wonderful. But, unless one species – humans – quickly changes its behavior, many of these precious species will disappear, some before we even discover them.

I hope that this book has introduced you to some amazing animals and encouraged you to take another look at a few species you thought you already knew. In knowing more about these creatures, I hope you might love them as I do and want to protect them and their homes, too.

Ben

# Glossary

**adaptations**
skills that an animal or plant has evolved over a long time to survive in its *habitat*

**aquatic**
an animal that grows or lives in or near water

**camouflage**
When animals are colored or patterned to match their surroundings. This helps them to hide from other animals.

**carbon dioxide**
An invisible gas with no smell that is necessary for life on Earth. When humans and animals breathe out, they release *carbon dioxide* into the air. Plants use it to make food.

**Carnivora**
a group of *mammals*, including cats and dogs, that have powerful jaws

**carnivore**
an animal that eats only other animals

**chemicals**
Substances that make up everything in the world around us. For example, *oxygen*.

**clotting**
when blood goes sticky and dry to stop a cut or wound from bleeding

**crustaceans**
a group of animals without a backbone and with a hard covering that mostly live in the water

**echolocation**
when an animal with very sensitive ears, such as a bat or a whale, finds its way around objects it cannot see by making special sounds that bounce off hard surfaces

**endangered**
animals at risk of disappearing from Earth forever

**evolve**
when animals and other living things change over long periods of time by passing on their most useful skills and traits

**extinct**
when the last animal in a *species* dies, and no more exist

**glands**
special body parts inside an animal that produce substances that help other body parts work, or that the animal releases into its surroundings

**habitat**
an animal's or plant's home

**infrared**
A type of light that humans cannot see, but that we can feel as heat. Some animals, such as vampire bats and mosquitoes, can use infrared to see.

**larva**
The first form of a growing animal or insect, before it changes to its final form. For instance, caterpillars are the larva of butterflies.

**mammal**
A warm-blooded animal that breathes air, has a backbone, and grows hair or fur. Female *mammals* make milk to feed their young.

**mate**
When two animals breed together, they are *mates*. This process is called mating.

**nerves**
*Nerves* send important information between the brain and different body parts.

**oxygen**
an invisible gas with no smell necessary for the survival of all plants and animals on Earth, as it is one of the main parts of the air we breathe

**predator**
an animal that hunts other animals

**prey**
an animal that is hunted, killed, and eaten by another animal

**reproduce**
When an animal or a plant makes more of its own kind. Many animals *reproduce* with a *mate*.

**reptilian**
an animal with a backbone that breathes air and has scales instead of hair or feathers

**salamander**
A lizard-like *vertebrate* that is related to frogs and toads, and can live on land or in water. A *salamander* has a long body and tail, and – unlike a lizard – smooth, shiny skin.

**scavenger**
an animal that eats dead or rotting animals or plants, and sometimes another animal's *prey*

**sense**
The five basic *senses* are sight, hearing, smell, taste, and touch. These *senses* provide important information about what's happening around an animal and inside its body.

**species**
a group of animals or plants that are the same or very similar, and can breed with each other to produce young

**territory**
the space an animal uses for feeding, breeding, or raising its young

**toxin**
a type of poison

**venomous**
an animal that produces and injects venom (a type of poison) to protect itself against *predators*, to kill *prey*, or to do both

**vertebrates**
animals with backbones

Ben Rothery is a detail-obsessed illustrator from Norwich, via Cape Town. He combines multiple processes to create intricate and delicate illustrations and repeating patterns, full of fine detail and vibrant color.

Much of Ben's work is inspired or informed by his love of nature – he grew up wanting variously to be a shark, a dinosaur, or David Attenborough crossed with Indiana Jones, but he settled on illustration as a way to bring those fantasies to life on paper.

Ben works from a small studio in London, which he shares with an unnecessarily large collection of very sharp pencils.